THE CRIME BOSS COLORING BOOK

MOST NOTORIOUS MAFIA BOSSES OF THE 20TH CENTURY

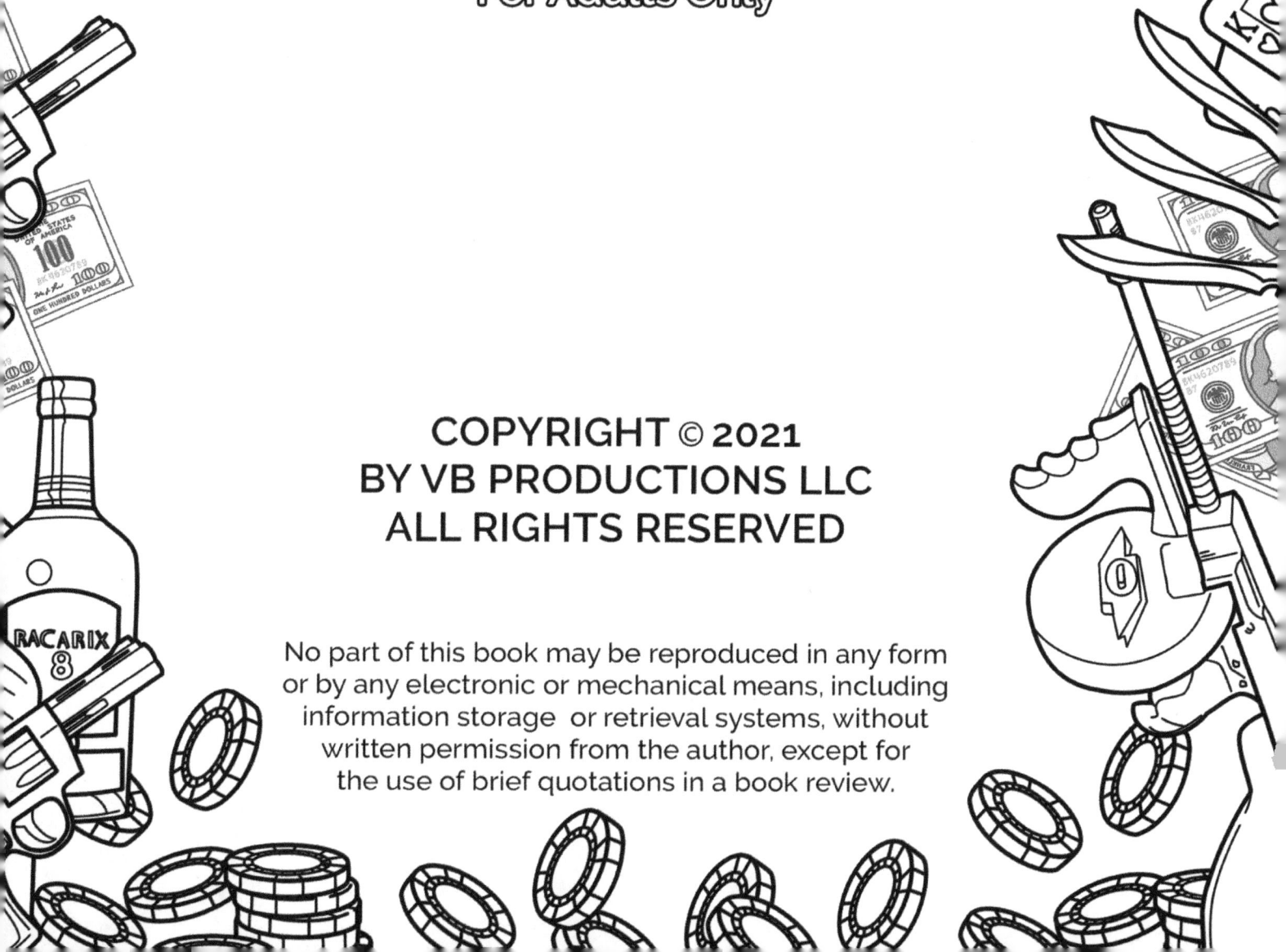

For Adults Only

COLOR TEST PAGE

A B C D
E F G
H I J
K L M
N O P
Q R S
T U V
W X Y Z

ALBERT ANASTASIA
Lord High
Executioner

CARLO GAMBINO The Godfather

CHARLES LUCIANO Lucky

FRANK COSTELLO
Prime Minister Of The Mob

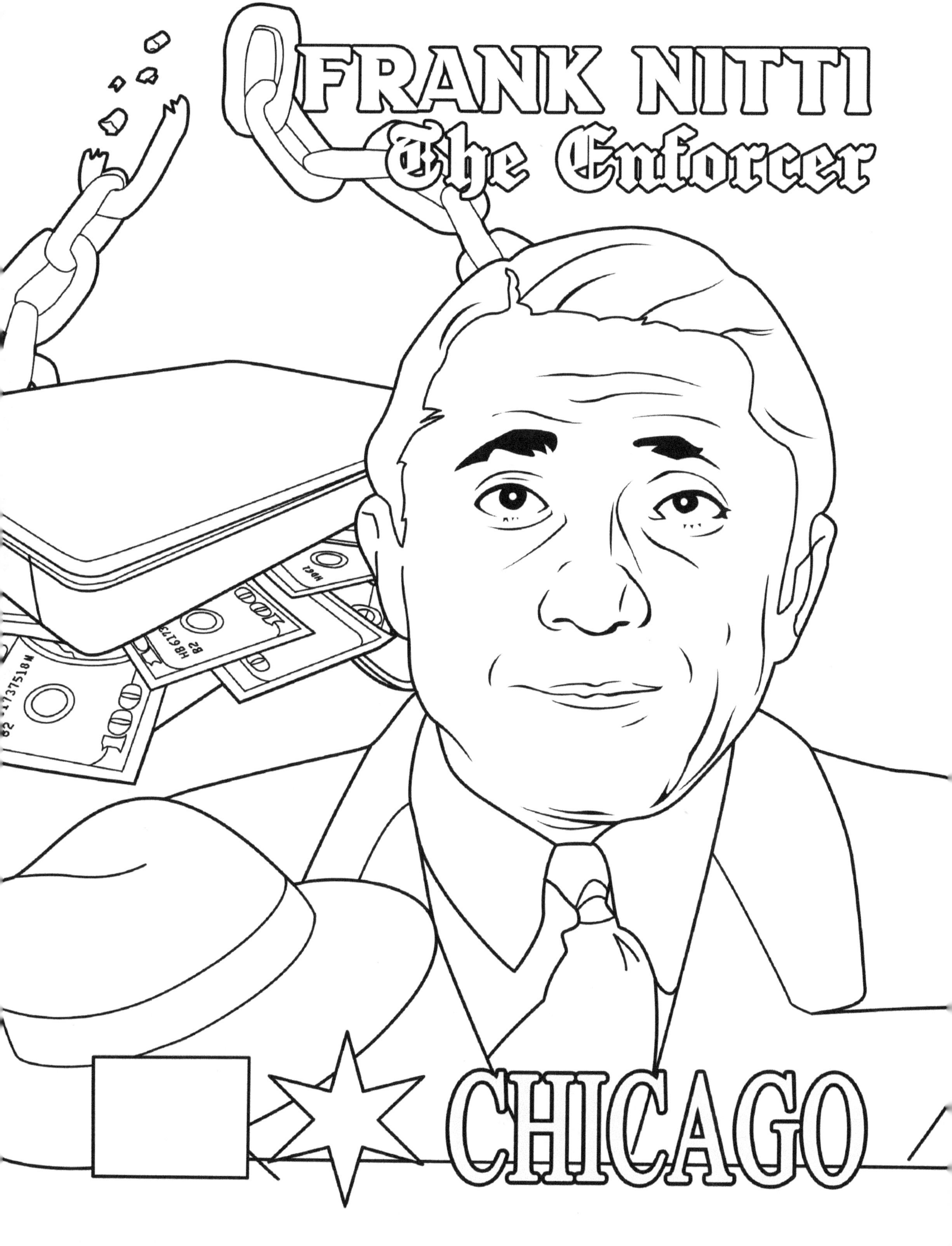
FRANK NITTI
The Enforcer
CHICAGO

JOE BONANNO
Joe Bananas

JOHN GOTTI
Teflon Don

JOHNNY TORRIO
The Fox

LOUIS BUCHALTER

Lepke

WANTED

LOUIS BUCHALTER LEPKE

PUBLIC ENEMY #1

$25,000 REWARD

MICKEY COHEN
King Of LA

30732
LA 7.18.33

HOLLYWOOD

SAM GIANCANA
Momo

TONY ACCARDO
Big Tuna

COUNTERFEIT

CHAIRMAN'S RESERVE

TOMMY LUCCHESE
Three-finger
Tommy Brown

www.ingramcontent.com/pod-product-compliance
Lightning Source LLC
Chambersburg PA
CBHW080631030426
42336CB00018B/3157